After
the Dome Fire

by Ruth Nolan

BAMBOO
DART
PRESS

LOS ANGELES † NEW YORK † LONDON † MELBOURNE

1st Runner-Up,
2021 Hillary Gravendyk Poetry Book Prize

_____

After the Dome Fire by Ruth Nolan

978-1-947240-63-6   Paperback

978-1-947240-64-3   eBook

Copyright © 2022 Ruth Nolan. All rights reserved.

First Printing 2022

Cover art by Dennis Callaci

Layout and design by Mark Givens

Several of the poems in this chapbook have been previously published in *Cholla Needles Magazine; Fire and Rain: Ecopoetry of California* (Scarlet Tanager); *Bad Ken; and San Diego Poetry Annual 2020-22.*

For information:

Bamboo Dart Press

chapbooks@bamboodartpress.com

Bamboo Dart Press 024

Pelekinesis
www.pelekinesis.com

BAMBOO DART PRESS
www.bamboodartpress.com

SHRiMPER
www.shrimperrecords.com

To my daughter Tarah and my grand-daughter Eve

Contents

Cima Dome
home of the largest Joshua tree forest
in the world

Mopping Up

It's the most unraveled and well-paying job I've had—
fighting fires in far-flung, fiery wilderness areas
in the San Bernardino Mountains, the San Gabriels,
the Sierra, Gates of the Wilderness, Trinity Alps.

Most of the time, I was the only girl on the crew,
cutting fireline, stumbling on rocks, sucking down smoke.

After a fire had laid down upon blackened meadows
And burnt-matchstick forests, our job was far from done.
We hiked through baked-potato-hot, ankle-deep ash
to finish off dying wildfires, using our sharpened shovels
to stir and sift through debris, slowly, oh so meticulously.

We joked that incinerated animals were crispy critters,
known in their former incarnations as Kangaroo rat,
Mojave Green rattlesnakes, Black-tailed jackrabbits.

We struggled to keep pace in the slowed-down underbelly
of once so lovely, if little known, Golden State geographies
with lonely names: Rattlesnake Mountain. Horse Thief Spring.
Last Chance Range. Grapevine Canyon. Wild Wash. Toro Peak.

Above us, whispered remains of trees lurking black and jagged,
stripped of the dignity of their names: Jeffrey Pines, Ponderosas
Western Sequoia. Sycamore. Pinyon. White Fir. Incense Cedar
now designated as widow makers, ready with death-blow limbs.

At our feet, the complete bequeathing of the ladder fuels—
Manzanita. Western Juniper. Coyote Brush. Poison Oak.

This is what I remember most vividly from my firefighting days:
the endless mopping up. Making sure the fire was put to bed.
Soothing feverish brows of forsaken landscapes to cool them down
Tame them into domiciled complicity with the ease of a nursery rhyme.

And I remember how often the guys on the crew would ask why I'd left
My apron strings of domesticity to flirt with fire instead of with them.

Fire Behavior

Hobo arsonists
dry lightning
exhaust pipes
weed whackers
illegal campfires
utility lines
gender reveal parties
epic drought
high winds
fatal heat
brittle plants
vertical terrain

fractious
combustion
champagne bottle explosions

people trying to escape
but nowhere to go

bluebirds
       warblers
           sparrows
plummet, aflame

the air, hot and thick as tar
blind evacuation
      fatal migration

Home Girl

The doctor yanked her from my womb,
turned her belly up to the light
that July night when thunderheads pillared
towards the glare of full desert moon.
Lightning strikes, the chances of wildfire,
but instead, the oddity of flash floods.

Because I have always inhabited deserts
I was not sure I could teach her how to swim.

Now, she is 11 years old, just beginning
to sprout little breasts that resemble
dorsal fins, this daughter whom I once
wished had been born a boy.

Each day, she asks me to hook the training bra
behind her back. She's a cool girl,
beautifying herself with beaded jewels,
skimpy skirts, platform shoes, green lip gloss
borrowed from god only knows who.

I have long since forgiven her
for the scar slashed across my lower gut,
the stingy kisses slurped across my cheek
the way fat mouthed fish gasp
for bugs hovering at the surface
on the scurvy Mojave River,

And each day, when she goes to school,
I sneak into her bedroom,
find the jars of teddy bear bottled nail polish
and with a surgeon's knife tip finesse
paint my own finger and toenails blue.
Sometimes I use red, the color of flames.

Making sure the fire is put to bed

TEUTONIA
PEAK
TRAIL

Burned Alive

This is where you are lost
When the cross at hilltop lights up
When the lone raven swirls above the ridge
When the hiker makes her lonely pilgrimage
When the sheep dog leads the way
When the bighorn sheep dance high on rocks
When rattlesnakes begin to stir in the singe
When the smoke tree blush into purple bloom
When the half-moon reveals her woman-song
When the sky to the east is half-pink
When the palm trees sigh in light wind
When coyotes cry and gather for the kill
Where skin melts away from flesh, tooth-torn
This is where the in-between worlds collide
This is where the desert and sea change guard
This is where time slows to a tortoise crawl
This is where you are found

Fire Poppies

You, with your untimely yellow heads
stealth bombers from coastal hills
hidden in plain sight
until someone sees you
and reveals your true name

Pretend you aren't causing harm
to the indigenous flora and fauna
that you won't make the sheep sick
that you won't scent up the land
with your exotic fragrances
you don't belong in the Mojave
when it looks like it's supposed to
with Joshua tree – Juniper woodlands
yet here, you thrive
fueling wildfires,
regenerating so easily
on scorched earth,
lover of flames.
You are invasive species.
Feeding on death.
Hated but here to stay.

Desert Rat

Hates cities and snow, cultivates shotguns
Refuses to talk about the old countries, NY, Ireland
builds an adobe house in a Joshua tree forest
then plants a sharp-barbed privacy windscreen
that also serves as a fence: Palo Verde and tamarisk
whose deep tap roots can never be completely dug up
then imports his wife and sons and daughter from L.A.
gives them old dirt bikes, never mind the promised horses
talks about making and selling rattlesnake belt bands
tells tales of gold buried out here, burns trash in the yard
has fun shooting at ravens and turkey vultures at dusk.

Understory
—teenage wasteland

Long days walking across the desert, nowhere to go. Police pulling up to ask for I.D. and letting her go too easily. Hitchhiking up and down Happy Trails Highway and Bear Valley Road, looking for a fast-food job. Father figures who pick her up to give her rides and offer money for *something to put in your mouth*. Lonely rock peaks. Bleached coyote skulls. Zigzagging jackrabbits. Visions of Moses and the burning bush, from Catholic school days. Creosote waving their psychedelic arms in the murder winds. Dust devils and mirage filtered through God-talking Joshua trees. Ravens and turkey vultures landing in wide washes at dusk. Sleeping on cabin roofs. Views of faraway freeway lights, a full-bellied moon. Blood sunrise. The eager dogs of dawn.

Devil's Hole

Pupfish, an exotic Mojave Desert fish
endangered, protected by federal laws,
surviving mass extinction for centuries
in just a few far flung oasis ponds
where temperatures rise in summers
to above 120 degrees
clinging to life in tiny ponds
scattered across the desert
along the course of dead-end rivers
broken up by freeways and towns
following the long shrinking of
historic inland lakes and rivers
whose waters now flow mostly underground.

The old rancher laughs.
Hell, we used to feed 'em to the cats.

Lightning Strike

I didn't want to see the scars
Someone hacked into the live oak tree

In Joshua Tree, in the monument
In the place where a fresh breeze

Blows up from the south, always

Today, humidity's lip,
Yesterday, my lover's hip
I touched a bruised sky.
Rain imagined
Rain on a walk
Rain on the dirt
Rain in a raven's beak
These hummingbirds,

How they haunt my ability to glide
Red zinger wings, black chinned,
The memory of wetter footsteps

Woolly mammoth, giant sloths

Somewhere lost
Where your eyes blind
Me to this place

Someone took an axe
Because they could

To the only tree
In the desert
Where dream trails collide
And fall apart
Re-draw the skin
Make a new map, acorns and shells
Someone else might find the way
Through these sand roots
It's not me, too committed
To a precise place
No one has named—
Yet, the promise of rain
The taste of rain, the smell
Heavy with creosote scent
It is pouring
And I am not wet
This tree, wetter now
Than last year
When the dying
Had just taken hold
Some special kind of nut
Shaken abruptly to the ground
Taking so long to crack apart

The air, hot and thick as tar

Westward, Ho

Compass Barrel cactus
crowning with yellow flowers

Jimson Weed blowing big to-do's
in the shapes of ghost trombones

wagon trains heading west
searching for water-source

orange poppies, sky-smoke
exploding at the head of the pass

it might be someone's birthday
celebrate with Mormon Tea

it might be a day to dig someone's grave
pound a cross into the ground.

China Ranch 1912

Because the baby died suddenly
almost making it until the end of summer
   she never cried
did anyone see who lit the flames?
when it happened
hired men harvesting dates from the palms
   they heard the children scream
at Tecopa that day
the temperature topped 117 degrees
by the next morning
beer bags had been packed
   no one waved good-bye
the train for Barstow pulled away
rain that night, first in months
heavy as lead shot, loud as screams
crashing down the canyon.

Barely There
27 Februaries ago + peyote tea

I hiked all the way to the top of East Ord Mountain
with three guys from the fire crew and a 12-pack of beer

Kevin, who made almost a million dollars
growing marijuana in a hydroponic greenhouse

Tom, my boyfriend, who was strictly vegetarian
He liked to take Volkswagen engine apart for fun

Vinnie, Native American but often mistaken
for Italian, future father of my daughter. We hiked

through a jagged landscape lacking trails
to the top of a lonely, 6,000 feet high mountain peak.

We took turns firing Vinnie's AK47 at rock outcrops.
    I cannot tell a lie. Shooting that rifle was a lot of fun.

And near the windy summit, we found a charred pair
of bighorn sheep horns resting near a cave, and they

looked centuries old. Probably burned from some fire
that swept through here after some old animal died.

Years later, a Chemehuevi elder tells me this:
Those horns were placed there as an offering by a shaman.

He cried for us all. He touched the stars.

My Daughter's Father

I should have loved him more than you
I used shovels, he ran chainsaw
He bought beer for the whole fire crew
I should have loved him more than you
Asked me out, nothing I could do
He brought me silver, bought it raw
I should have loved him more than you
I used shovels, he ran chainsaw.

Lying Down
—a flirtation with Edward Abbey

All spring, the dreary wind blows
Me, here, the fairer sex, a lovely yellow wildflower
Rattlesnakes, pink and thick, hiding in the shade
The little water holes, bitter springs
And in the midst of this fairy tale symphony, they arrive—
The sun, a pale cadaver roaring at you all day
Two flat tires, not enough water, the last tin of tuna
Rock falls of unknown origin, scurrying on little claws
The loner, following you back on the trail from Devil's Hole
The drunk man pulling a gun on you on Granite Peak
The Army Ranger boyfriend at home, loading his guns
Why? The rain that comes down like lead shot and wrecks the trail
Quicksand lapping at your crotch. The canyons like catacombs.
the pale cadaver of a ten-inch centipede.
Lonely peaks with name like Mollie's Nipple
It is not possible
That the rabbit loves the owl.

Soothing the feverish brows of forsaken landscapes
to help cool them down, shovel-stir

Willis Palms

The fire of 2010 torched all the palms
Matchstick heads, ridiculous skin bodies
They all burned up together, a family of fronds
A fire ignited by a Thanksgiving arsonist
Ten years later, it's all grown back
Burn-marked bodies with greened-up heads
Many more hordes of tourists here now
This story is spelled out over and over again
The ceremony of crucifixion, sacrificial lambs
Just like this, a herd of elephant skins
Tromping through wet marshlands
Nourished by their wet footprints
Undulating, then reposing in the sand
In the folds of bitter-sun hills

This Is the Largest Joshua Tree Forest in the World
—says a sign in the middle of the 25,000 acre Dome Fire burn zone

After the before song
After this
A domed landscape of Joshua trees torn up by a firestorm
After this
The high ridge for agave collecting has burned to a crisp
After this
It has been years since you saw a desert tortoise crawl
After this
The ruby-throated hummingbirds desperate with thirst
After this
A young chuckwalla doesn't back down from its fierce rock
After this
The long-eared owls, claiming their only tree, portending death
After this
The rattlesnake shaman's circle, so hard to see it makes you cry
After this
The heat is killing more people this year than ever before
After this
The tender landscape, fragile and fragmented in broken light
After this
People-songs, one trail leading to and from another broken start
After this
The fluid memory song in the cottonwood oasis where someone died
After this
The first and only evening star, remembered long before its white heart

Streamers
Shine on, you crazy diamond

Wee Thump Wilderness, on the desert's eastern ridge
Joshua trees twist to the sky. Some are over 600 years old.

At Ivanpah nearby, 500-feet high solar tracking towers
blind the sky, dominating valley and mountains east and west.

In Paiute, "Wee Thump" means *ancient ones*. Respect for age.
"Ivanpah" means *place of white clay*. Relationship with source.

Below, thousands of acres of mirrors reflect the sun
crushing endangered California desert tortoise habitats

attracting large birds of prey – bald eagles, condors –
who mistake it for water and instead burst into flames,

incinerating on the spot. Workers at Ivanpah are mostly
young and they have a funny name for this, *streamers*

Lovers and gamblers speed along Interstate 15 nearby
to get married or divorced, hit a jackpot on the first slot.

Backburn

They go farther for wood
deeper for the yellow metal
that makes white men crazy
they burn the rabbits out
from wide meadows of sagebrush
on the other side of barbed wire fence
they say it's to protect their crops
I am here, shadowing the
spirit world, remembering wildflower
ceremonies each spring, picking
stems one by one
scattering seeds
on this madman's disconnect
burnishing my name and yours
onto our tarnished land
with the intent of flame
to bring back all of creation
back together again.

Escape Route

My little daughter and I are back from a few years up in Shoshone
pounding family pictures to the walls of our apartment in Joshua Tree

Not far from where my daughter's father shot and killed his best friend.
He went to prison, sentenced to life in prison, working on fire camp crews.

I'll claim the desk I left in his parents' garage when I left town last time
A well-made oak apparition cracked by the heat, but useful nonetheless

I'll sand the surface with a razor to reveal a deeper truth in the grain
Shining, beautiful stories I want my daughter to inherit someday.

Did anyone
see who lit
the flames?

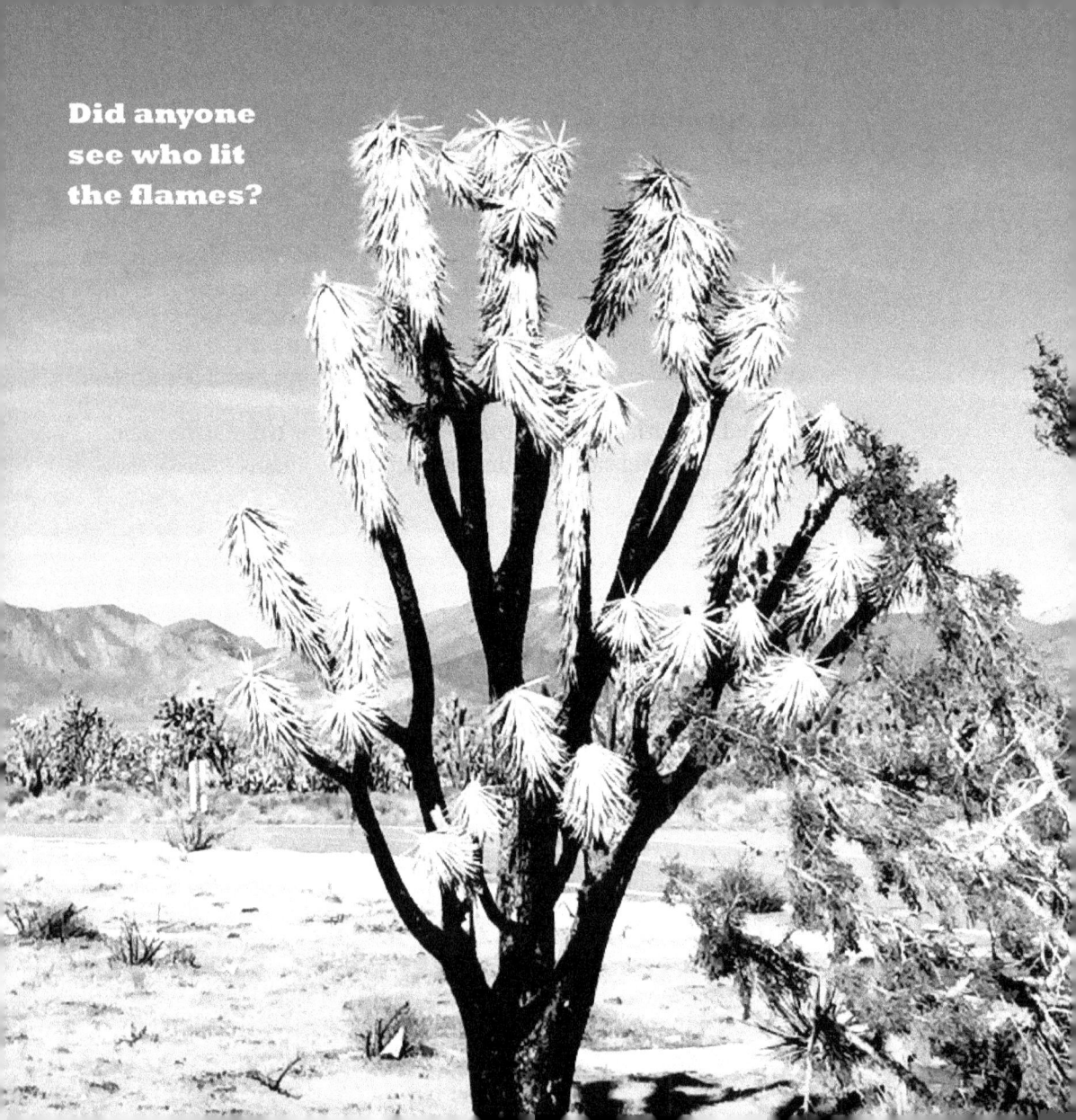

Ghost Flower
—for Mary Beal, desert botanist

Shivering by day, glowing at night

blooming only in early spring, this wildflower

identifiable by splotches of red bound by a white heart

attracting lovers through mimicry, not actually producing nectar

named by a woman botanist working alone in the Mojave

to render it bold and known

this small flower speaks with a lisp on rocky lips, forsaken cliffs

flourishing where no woman should go

but there she is, forever hard to find, unless you tiptoe by

Sun Dog

He comes to charge my car battery
says he has a thing for teachers with glasses
I hesitate to let him remove my clothes
he offers to give me a back massage outside
on the short grass by the pool
    if I would just lie face-down on the floor
    he'll rub in the cheap sunscreen
    so my exposed skin
    doesn't get burned
I tell him he's lucky to have a wife
I am tired of living alone so I pretend I don't
his hands are strong from pulling engines apart
and feel like afternoon sunshine on my skin
the Santa Ana winds of incendiary October
tear at slats of wood in the backyard fence
and the sky manages to look like rain
for a tiny desert in this emptiest of landscapes
and so, I surrender to something
that feels like love
but is not.

Fire Lookout

The famous architect, contemplating his biography
he had built a comfortable house in hell made of cinderblock
white sugary cubes accentuating its lines
imported water drawn from mountains miles away
that once sustained an entire Native American tribe
to fill the pool, water the lawn
    because who would live in the desert without a pool?
admitting that the only reasons for building here
(where every life form seeks shelter during unbearable daylight hours)
is to let mad dogs and rich men go out in the noon sun
let them own and dominate a view they admire
observed from the wide walls of floor to ceiling windows
of a sharp-angled structure not fitting the country
but challenging it. This, his Garden of the World.

    —after Wallace Stegner, *The American West as Living Space*

Friendly Fire

The attic door opened easily
that pearl smooth August night
after a day spent hitchhiking
on washboard roads, nothing hard

One push, we climbed on the roof
two sunburned, runaway teenage girls
a backpack full of cheese and fruit
stolen from the market that day

We'd broken into a desert cabin.
I shot a window with my father's gun.
No one had been there for a long time
the refrigerator was propped open.

We crawled through splintered glass.
You worried that there might be
a dead baby or rattlesnake inside.
I found an unopened bottle of wine.

I held the buck knife, and you held
the fruit. I sliced the salami and
licked my sticky fingers, then you
twisted the corkscrew and laughed.

We sifted through the box of jewels
stolen from our moms. You clasped
a silver necklace on my burnt neck
and I slipped an old ring onto you.

We shared an old wool army blanket
and a man's extra-large flannel shirt
talked about all the guys we shared
cock and breast size, abortion cramps.

You wanted to know what it was like
to fight fires; I told you I had no sisters.
I popped the cork, you passed the bottle
I thought I could taste your tongue

delivered like the silent rise of moon
punctuating spaces between stars
I watched Venus, Orion's Belt fade
while you spread oysters onto rye.

White Hot Manhunt

This broken love story
was told by a teenaged girl
by owners of the Inn at the Oasis
by the first established
white woman pioneer,
by the Disney cartoonist
who built a cabin
on the other side
of the mountains
from hand-hewn palms
by the Indian agent
whose last name
was True, by the
San Bernardino Sun,
by the desert scholar
by a family member
by the Raven circling
above, by the National
Park Service, by
the university historian,
by a 100th anniversary playwright
by the surviving family
by the rusted shotgun
at the bottom of the sag pond
by the New York Times,
by the date palm farmer

by the sheriff's posse
by an indigenous elder
by the Palm Springs Museum
by people in a writing workshop
by the blogger, by the
residents of Pahrump
by the drifter who torched
the last of the 29 Palms
on the windiest night of the year
if this is not love, what is

At our feet
the complete bequeathing of ladder fuels

Of the Mojave
—for Mary Austin

Of little rain
the two-step of motherhood
in a most arid place
breaking water
gushing membranes
void of life, then violent
when all the earth
cries, its whole duty
to flower
and bear fruit—
to underestimate one's thirst
in this land

Widow Maker
—Those branches hanging from burnt trees, ready to fall on someone's head

So, we could be driving together to Forest Falls
Sweltering our way to the water songs at the creek
Then jumping, shocked, then invigorated by the cold,
Escaping an impossibly hot summer day down below.

We could be standing in the cool rain at South Fork
Having pulled off the busy highway at the first drops
Laughing when it starts to hail, our clothes getting wet.
From 110 to 69 degrees, just like that. We got away.

We could be irritated by the slow motorcycle up ahead
Frustrated at Onyx Summit, traffic far to slow, impatient
Deciding not to stop at the lake, too many people, this
Awful pandemic. We'd drive farther out, rip off the masks.

We could be racing through deep mud holes, splashing,
Not a care that tomorrow, the underbelly of the car
Will be caked with hard dirt. We'd drive a little reckless,
Knowing we were still in control. We'd have fun.

We would most definitely live at the edge, and be okay,
Taking the tight turns and mudholes in race-car mode
Because neither of us can stand monotony, being bored
We would take such risks on this narrow, steep road.

We could be standing at Old Jim's grave, add another
Beer can to the pile, we'd explore the ruins of old miners'
Dreams up here, at the meadow, the old cabin now home
To rats and snakes. We'd feel a little spooky, seeing how

Final and how un-erasable this feeling of life and death,
Hovering side by side in Holcomb Valley on a hot day,
Thick smoke from statewide wildfires, realizing there is
No escape from this. We could be together, seeking beauty,

Finding beauty in harsh terrain, painting our world again.
We could watch the sunset, hauntingly orange this eve,
We could be best of friends again, never mind the wildfires
Or heat, or tragedies upon tragedy: why do you have to be dead.

Furnace Creek

We are women of the desert
We have been here since time began
We have taken care of the water, our life source
Burning away weeds seasonally to keep our springs clean
Until we were pushed out to live in the sand
We saw those people from the Manly Party in 1849
They refused to speak with us
This is our place of life, a place of renewal
Their name for this place, "Death Valley," is unfortunate
We live as one with the valleys, mountains, flats, meadows, springs
All of water is interconnected across the desert
We have been the keepers of the springs for centuries
We don't separate from what is part of us

Smoke Tree

Scarification—

the process

by which you are born

after the water-surge

of flash flood

leaves you exposed

thin shoulder seed

you ache with song

boulder brutalities

scraping winds

from the east

lift you up

from the dry wash

into puffs of mint smoke

signifying fire

but not here

When we mother
Our tormented
landscapes

Good Fire

I have traveled deeply
into your perfect body
swallowed whole veins
carried you away
in my deep pockets
ground you into dust
never mind the strip mines
the gutted hillsides
after all else burned
and been stripped away
a strange new beauty
will flourish here
Buckwheat
Manzanita
Spineflower
Bladderpod
each underwatered bloom
its own perfect dry moon

Fire Regime

This is where you are lost, deep in the Mojave
Where Joshua trees shed their charred skin

When the lone raven swirls above the ridge
Where the hiker makes her lonely pilgrimage

Where the bighorn sheep dance high on rocks
Where charred cholla cacti bare black arms

When rattlesnakes begin to stir from dens
When the indigo-bush beads into blue bloom

When the half-moon reveals her woman-song
When the sky to the east is half-pink

Where burnt matchstick palms weep with soot
When the canyon ahead is peopled with rocks

When coyotes cry and gather for the kill
This is where the in-between worlds collide

This is where the desert and sea change guard
This is where time slows to a low tortoise crawl

This is where the western Jay picks through scars
This is where lupine burns a brighter purple

This is where the sacred places reveal themselves
After the fire has swept through. You are found.

Teaching My Daughter to Put Out Fire

It isn't your typical scenario
a young mother, who worked
seven years ago as a wildland firefighter
driving a jeep in four-wheel drive
up 3N14, the back road to Big Bear
with her daughter five years old
to reach the Rattlesnake Fire burn zone
the last fire she ever fought.
This is another July day.

The mother wants to see for herself
how the mangled landscape looks today,
what remains of the Joshua and Pinyon trees
what bird sounds filter now through barren air
what reference points to negotiate by
without the Jeffrey Pines or live oak
without the juniper and
she worked on this fire
she watched it burn away
huge boulder-scatter revealed
ominous ghost-whales
rising from the heavy smoke

She wants to re-assess, look for signs of life
Now that so much has been taken away
one careless toss of a cigarette
one careless finger on a trigger
a father locked away, his best friend dead.
Some things have been destroyed forever.

It might be a day to dig someone's grave,
pound a cross into a rock

Some things have been saved.
Some things new and strange grow in this space.

Will there be birds? Ravens? Western Jay?
Will there be mountain wildflowers, suckling
the darkened dirt? Perhaps a few deer,
negotiating their way across a moonscape
on their way to a small spring. Jackrabbits
hopping in and out of the slowly dying
and grotesquely regrowing Joshua trees.

Before they reach the lonely place,
they stop at an empty campground
so the daughter can run and play.
Her daughter spots it first: a wisp of smoke
tickled by the light wind and rising.
a careless camper, a campfire not put out.
The mother reaches for her Army shovel
and hands her daughter a bottle of water.

We have work to do
this is how you put a fire
before it has a chance to erupt—
look for the small things
a wisp of sultry smoke
a gleam of orange eyes
a seduction of tiny flame
this is where it starts
this is where it will stop
nothing more will burn here today.

About the Author

Ruth Nolan grew up in California's Mojave Desert and worked as a wildland firefighter for the Bureau of Land Management's California Desert District and also for the U.S. Forest Service, fighting wildfires throughout the western U.S. Her writing is forthcoming in *Writing the Golden State: The New Literary Terrain of California* (Angel City Press) and has been notably published in *Boom, California; McSweeney's; East Bay Times; Joshua Tree: Where Two Deserts Meet* (Wildsam Guide); *Los Angeles Fiction: Southland Writing by Southland Writers* (Red Hen Press); *Desert Oracle; Nevada Independent* and *Coachella Review*. Ruth also writes for *News from Native California; Inlandia Literary Journeys; KCET Artbound L.A.* and *KCET Tending Nature*.

Ruth is Professor of English and creative writing at College of the Desert. She is curator of the humanities project *Fire on the Mojave: Stories from the Deserts and Mountains of Inland Southern California*, and editor of the critically acclaimed anthology, *No Place for a Puritan: the Literature of California's Deserts* (Heyday.) Ruth was named the inaugural Mojave Desert Literary Laureate in 2021.

BAMBOO DART PRESS

112 N. Harvard Ave. #65
Claremont, CA 91711

chapbooks@bamboodartpress.com
www.bamboodartpress.com

www.ingramcontent.com/pod-product-compliance
Lightning Source LLC
Chambersburg PA
CBHW081651270326
41933CB00018B/3431